NICSHELLE A. F.

Motivational Philosophy Workbook

Creativity of a Genius
Teacher of the Year Series

*Transportation

NICSHELLE A. FARROW M.A.Ed

Future Juris Doctor

NICSHELLE A. FARROW Future Juris Doctor

Copyright © 2019 Nicshelle A. Farrow M.A.Ed

All rights reserved.

ISBN:
ISBN-13:

DEDICATION

To people involved with caring for the world on all levels.

NICSHELLE A. FARROW Future Juris Doctor

CONTENTS

	Acknowledgments	ii
1	Introduction	4
2	Transportation	5-9
3	Before School	10-14
4	During School	15-19
5	After School	20-26
6	Thoughts	27-29
7	Word Work	30-79
8	Phrase Work	80-87
9	Sentence Work	88-100
10	About the Author	101-102

ACKNOWLEDGMENTS

Thank you to all of my family and entities that have supported my plight to increase literacy worldwide and who continues to share my books and mantra, GoDaWork for Goodwill.

NICSHELLE A. FARROW Future Juris Doctor

Introduction

The following sections provide thought provoking words, phrases, and sentences.

The purpose is to motivate students to honor their intellectual property, ponder more strategically by writing and sketching about their opinion(s) on paper.

Ultimately, the goal of this series is to inspire and elevate growth mindsets for the hope that people who will fill the lines of each workbook will in turn enrich more growth mindsets.

Motivational speaking engagements will encompass the following words, phrases, sentences, and philosophy.

1 TRANSPORTATION

The state of moving from one destination to another to accomplish task(s) is a step in the right direction. To win anything, most often people must arrive via a medium of transportation.

Reflection

- **Visualize**
- **Intellectual Celebration**
- **Reread**
- **Attitude Enrichment**
- **List Ideas/Concepts/Words**

_____
_____
_____
_____
_____
_____
_____
_____
_____
_____

Design a Stage On Paper to Showcase Your Reflection.

Then, write your detailed goals while sharing why you selected specific goals.

_____

_____

_____

_____

_____

_____

_____

_____

_____

_____

_____

_____

_____

_____

_____

_____

Thereafter, create an action plan to produce and market a product(s) from your intellectual property.

_____

_____

_____

_____

_____

_____

_____

_____

_____

_____

_____

_____

_____

_____

2 BEFORE SCHOOL

Pensively thinking is a trait of masters of arts. Thinking has become an art. The art of questioning to provoke thinking is masterful. To project accomplishments from the time spent in planning from the minds of a mastermind tank has become exuberantly valuable to billions of people.

Reflection:

- **Visualize**
- **Intellectual Celebration**
- **Reread**
- **Attitude Enrichment**
- **List Ideas/Concepts/Words**

_____
_____
_____
_____
_____
_____
_____
_____
_____
_____

Design a Stage
On Paper to Showcase Your Reflection.

Then, write your detailed goals while sharing why you selected specific goals.

_____

_____

_____

_____

_____

_____

_____

_____

_____

_____

_____

_____

_____

_____

_____

_____

_____

Thereafter, create an action plan to produce and market a product(s) from your intellectual property.

3 DURING SCHOOL

Internal motivation is a must and not a need in order to be ambitious about anything!

Reflection:
- **Visualize**
- **Intellectual Celebration**
- **Reread**
- **Attitude Enrichment**
- **List Ideas/Concepts/Words**

Design a Stage
On Paper to Showcase
Your Reflection.

Then, write your detailed goals while sharing why you selected specific goals.

Thereafter, create an action plan to produce and market a product(s) from your intellectual property.

4 AFTER SCHOOL

Reflection, application, verbalization of information to process a written summation, and follow-up is a program needed consistently after a session of learning.

Reflection:

- **Visualize**
- **Intellectual Celebration**
- **Reread**
- **Attitude Enrichment**
- **List Ideas/Concepts/Words**

_____
_____
_____
_____
_____
_____
_____
_____
_____
_____

Then, write your detailed goals while sharing why you selected specific goals.

_____

_____

_____

_____

_____

_____

_____

_____

_____

_____

_____

_____

_____

_____

_____

_____

_____

ABC's

Design a Stage
On Paper to Showcase
Your Reflection.

Thereafter, create an action plan to produce and market a product(s) from your intellectual property.

_____
_____
_____
_____
_____
_____
_____
_____
_____
_____
_____
_____
_____
_____
_____
_____
_____
_____
_____
_____

ABC's

Thoughts

Thinking is critical.

What are your thoughts?

The above question is indicative of respect for a person's intellectual property not yet shared.

Thoughts!

Thoughts!

Thoughts!

Let optimistic thoughts lead to healthy and productive action.

Why not share your thoughts?

Indeed, protect your intellectual property first and foremost unless the time and mind permits thoughts to be shared for free.

Once upon a time, I learned that information is a commodity.

Write to share your concept of the word:

Thinking

Write to share your concept of the word:

Perseverance

Write to share your concept of the word:

Dreamer

_____
_____
_____
_____
_____
_____
_____
_____
_____
_____
_____
_____

Write to share your concept of the word:

Accomplishments

Write to share your concept of the word:

Attitude

_____

_____

_____

_____

_____

_____

_____

_____

_____

_____

_____

_____

Write to share your concept of the word:

Potential

_____
_____
_____
_____
_____
_____
_____
_____
_____
_____
_____
_____
_____

Write to share your concept of the word:

Confidence

Write to share your concept of the word:

Clarity

Write to share your concept of the word:

Challenges

Write to share your concept of the word:

Focus

Write to share your concept of the word:

Courage

Write to share your concept of the word:

Risks

Write to share your concept of the word:

Determination

Write to share your concept of the word:

Imagination

Write to share your concept of the word:

Patience

Write to share your concept of the word:

Forgiveness

Write to share your concept of the word:

Gratitude

_____

_____

_____

_____

_____

_____

_____

_____

_____

_____

_____

_____

_____

_____

Write to share your concept of the word:

Goals

Write to share your concept of the word:

Hope

Write to share your concept of the word:

Robotic

Write to share your concept of the word:

Success

Write to share your concept of the word:

Tenacious

Write to share your concept of the word:

Youthful

Write to share your concept of the word:

Leadership

Write to share your concept of the word:

Motivated

Write to share your concept of the word:

Trustworthy

Write to share your concept of the word:

Enthusiasm

Write to share your concept of the word:

Teachable

Write to share your concept of the word:

Ambitious

_____

_____

_____

_____

_____

_____

_____

_____

_____

_____

_____

_____

Write to share your concept of the word:

Priorities

_____
_____
_____
_____
_____
_____
_____
_____
_____
_____
_____
_____
_____

Write to share your concept of the word:

Momentum

Write to share your concept of the word:

Energetic

Create a poem for the following phrase:

Future-Forward

Create a poem for the following phrase:

Focus-Driven

Create a poem for the following phrase:

Thought-Provoking

Create a poem for the following phrase:

Success-Driven

Create a poem for the following phrase:

Make Moves

Create a poem for the following phrase:

Music Speaks

Create a poem for the following phrase:

Growth Mindset

_____

_____

_____

_____

_____

_____

_____

_____

_____

_____

_____

_____

Create a poem for the following phrase:

Window of Opportunity

Exercise think time and write to support future entrepreneurs from the context of the following sentence:

From the bottom to the top, it can be achieved.

Exercise think time and write to support future entrepreneurs from the context of the following sentence:

Take advantage of the window of opportunity.

_____
_____
_____
_____
_____
_____
_____
_____
_____
_____
_____

Exercise think time and write to support future entrepreneurs from the context of the following sentence:

There is nothing like a win-win situation.

Exercise think time and write to support future entrepreneurs from the context of the following sentence:

Having a million dollar mind is something to reckon with.

_____
_____
_____
_____
_____
_____
_____
_____
_____
_____
_____

Exercise think time and write to support future entrepreneurs from the context of the following sentence:

Where is the fruit from your acquired skills?

_____
_____
_____
_____
_____
_____
_____
_____
_____
_____

Exercise think time and write to support future entrepreneurs from the context of the following sentence:

Two heads are better than one.

_____
_____
_____
_____
_____
_____
_____
_____
_____
_____

Exercise think time and write to support future entrepreneurs from the context of the following sentence:

Why not take a chance on winning?

_____
_____
_____
_____
_____
_____
_____
_____
_____

Exercise think time and write to support future entrepreneurs from the context of the following sentence:

What will you do with the fruits of your labor?

_____
_____
_____
_____
_____
_____
_____
_____
_____

ABOUT THE AUTHOR

Nicshelle Farrow is an educator of K-Adult Education thus far.

She has a Master's of Arts Degree in Education Administration Supervision. Nicshelle is a certified clear credentialed teacher in the state of California and also holds certification in Montessori Education for primary grades. She has worked for public, charter, private, adult, and Montessori schools.

Nicshelle is also the Education Director for the Universal Hip Hop Museum for the West Coast and the C.E.O of Journey To Stardom Productions that provides advertisement for entertainers. She also holds acting classes online and in-person. In addition, Nicshelle is a social media strategist for a plethora of other nonprofit organizations as a community advocate.

Nicshelle is a networking machine. She networks under many hats that she wears as a filmmaker, photographer, actress, comedian, radio personality, red carpet events' host, author, scriptwriter, motivational speaker, advertisement consultant, film, and literary editor. Nicshelle enjoys being creative, learning, teaching, and providing platforms to exercise creativity.

EDUCATION & CREDENTIALS

M.A.Ed University of Phoenix, Henderson, Nevada 2008

B.A. University of Dominguez Hills, Carson, California 2001

A.A. Community College of Southern Nevada, Las Vegas, Nevada 1992

North American Montessori Center Diploma

Pi Lambda Theta, National Education Society

Made in the USA
Middletown, DE
25 November 2022